The Buy to Let Landlords' Guide to Finding Great Tenants

David Lawrenson

First published 2016
All rights reserved

Copyright © David Lawrenson, 2016

David Lawrenson is hereby identified as the author of this work in accordance with Section 77 of the Copyright, Designs and Patents Act 1988.

ISBN-13: 978-1542316910
ISBN-10: 154231691X

INTRODUCTION 1

About Me 2

How This Book Is Structured 3

CHAPTER 1 - LETTING THROUGH A LETTING AGENT 7

High Street v Online Letting Agent 9

What does a High Street Letting Agent Do? 13

CHAPTER 2 - FINDING TENANTS YOURSELF 27

Step One - Marketing Your Property 28

The Screening-to-Move in Process 35

About the References and Steps to Move in Date 46

CHAPTER 3 - THE SPECIAL SITUATIONS 52

Letting to House Sharers (Including Students) 53

Renting a Shared House - HMOs and the rules on Licensing and Health and Safety 54

Letting to Local Authorities, Housing Associations and Other Government Agencies 57

Letting Directly to Tenants on Housing Benefit / Local Housing Allowance / Universal Credit 67

APPENDIX - "ABOUT THE PROPERTY AND THE CONTRACT" 75

Introduction

This book is all about how to find good tenants.

It will ...

- Tell you how to find the right kind of people who will look after your property well, who will pay the rent on time and who will tell you promptly if anything needs fixing.

- Help you avoid the types of people who may be late with their rent (or not pay it at all) and who may annoy neighbours with late night parties and the like.

- Explain the best marketing methods to use to find the right tenants quickly, whether you are letting an exclusive apartment or a budget flat and whether you are letting to executives, students, people who are dependent on benefits to pay their rent or even if you are simply letting a room in your own home.

- Look at the pros and cons of using a high street letting agent to find your tenant or whether you should do it yourself. (Yes, you can! I will explain how). And if you want to do it yourself, it will show you how to do that to.

This book does not cover holiday lettings or very short term lets of the kind that companies like Airbnb provide. Neither is it intended to be an in depth guide to being a landlord, though it does highlight all the things you need to have in place before you can legally let a property. *(For an in-depth guide to how to be a landlord, including where and what type of property you* *should buy as well as a comprehensive guide to the legal requirements that us landlords have to comply with, readers should get my best selling property book, "Successful Property Letting - How to Make Money in Buy to Let" and check out my website at **www.LettingFocus.com**).*

My website **www.LettingFocus.com** also has lots of useful information for landlords, including a blog, occasional offers on products and services for landlords and it's also where you can also sign up for my newsletter.

About Me

After university and my MBA, I worked in financial services as an internal consultant and project manager, whilst moonlighting as a residential landlord. I let out my first place - a room in my flat - in 1985.

In 2002, my landlord business was so successful that I was able to stop working for other people to concentrate on being a full-time property investor. Then in 2005, the first edition of my book, *"Successful Property Letting - How to Make Money in Buy to Let"* came out and within 3 months, it had become the UK's top selling property book. It still is. I'm also author of a book for tenants called *"Tenants' Guide to Successful Renting"* which came out in 2016.

My views on the private rented sector are quoted regularly in national newspapers like *"The Times"* and the *"Daily Telegraph"* and in hundreds of property magazines and buy to let websites.

I am a regular speaker at trade shows and for public and private organisations and trade associations. I have advised the London Assembly and have spoken at the Council of Mortgage Lenders.

I also run a consultancy business. Through my consulting work I advise other landlords and any business that's involved in the private rented sector, whether directly or as a supplier.

Landlords who want more help than is contained in this book are welcome to visit **LettingFocus.com** and contact me at **david@LettingFocus.com**. At LettingFocus.com, you can find out more about my one to one advice service and seminars for landlords and join my free quarterly newsletter.

How This Book Is Structured

This book is structured so that people can dip in and out, but I think it is best that you read all of it at some point.

For example, if you are dead set on using a high street letting agent, you could still benefit from reading the sections on how to find tenants yourself (i.e. without using a high street letting agent) because it is good to know in more detail, what things a high street letting agent *should* be doing around the business of referencing tenants. Why? Because you need to know they are doing their job properly.

And if you don't think you want to let to people who are dependent on housing benefit, it won't take long to read the section that covers these types of lets too. It might just change your mind. And you might be surprised to hear that you can let to a housing association or council in some areas and get a guaranteed rent, even if the property is empty.

Then there are lettings to students - another potentially attractive area. I look at the ways to find tenants in this highly seasonal market too. If you are letting room-by-room or just letting one room in your own house, there are certain special ways to go about doing that right too. I'll explain all.

So, I suggest you read all of this book, so you can begin to consider different markets as potential opportunities. "Go on, go on" as Mrs. Doyle (of *Father Ted* fame) used to say. "Have a nice cup of tea and read the whole thing. And now, I'm not forcing you now, am I?" (OK, people who are not Father Ted fans won't have a clue what I'm on about here, so. I'll move on).

Let's now look at the main structure of this book.

In Chapter One, I look at how to let using a high street letting agent. I briefly consider the differences between high street letting agents and what I shall refer to in this book as "online letting agents". Then I go on to ask what it is that a high street letting agent should be doing for you - and how to choose a good one. I list lots of questions that you should be asking a letting agent, so you can figure out if they are good. In particular, I highlight the extreme importance of checking the contract you have with the letting agent and why you should not be scared to amend it in your favour and finally I look at negotiating the fee they are going to charge (and hopefully getting it lower or at least, getting more value for the same fee).

In Chapter Two, I look at how you can find a tenant yourself by using an online letting agent. There are lots of online agents around and their services are quite similar (as are their prices which are a lot lower than those charged by a high street letting agent). The main purpose of using an online letting agent is to get your property on the big portals like Rightmove and Zoopla where tenants can see it, but using an online letting agent means you'll have to do a lot of the rest of the work that a high street agent would otherwise do. I show how you can buy the online agent's add-on services to do referencing, take photos etc., but I think the best approach is to do everything else yourself. So, I will show you how you can do everything else a high street letting agent does as part of their "tenant find and move in" service. It's not hard if you have the time.

In Chapter Three, I look at how to find tenants in other more "specialised situations". The special situations include letting to students, letting to people in shared houses (which might include students, of course), letting room by room and letting to people who are dependent on housing benefits to pay their rent. These special situations use a lot of the same marketing approaches to find tenants as any other type of let - however, there are a few subtle differences of approach and challenges that you should be aware of. Also, there are some specialist websites that are worth considering too. In this third section, I look at long lease schemes wherein you can let a property for a long period to bodies like housing associations and councils and get guaranteed rent paid to you, even when your property is empty.

But before we blast into orbit, a quick word on taking the easy path - letting to friends.

Should you let to friends?

The answer is nearly always a big resounding "No". Move on, next topic. OK, you want more?

The fact is you should *never* do business with friends, at least not those friends you really value. The only exception to this might be where your friends are also people you have worked with in business, if you are self-employed and they are also self-employed businesspeople too. In that special case they will hopefully understand that "business is business" and not look for favours from you.

Otherwise don't do it, because friends will expect you to give them "mates rates" or for you to overlook it when they have left the property in a filthy condition at the end of a tenancy.

If you are serious about being a landlord, this kind of tolerance cannot be expected. You need to get a fair, (by which I mean a near-to-market) rent. You are not in the business of subsidising pals. Why should you? After all, do your friends expect to be paid less than market rates for the work that they do? No, they don't and neither should they expect you to give them property on the cheap.

The best approach to take when you are asked to let a property to a friend is to say you don't have one available but you'd be more than happy to help them in their quest for a suitable property using all the techniques set out in this book. As you will know what good landlords should be doing, you can help them by looking at things from the tenants' point of view, so that your friends don't end up paying excessive fees to letting agents and they manage to secure the very best property they can at the cheapest rent possible.

By doing this, you are giving them your knowledge - they are your friends after all. But you don't owe them a place to live in, nor do you owe yourself (or them) the stress of being their landlord. Friendship only extends so far. So, keep your friend by not becoming their landlord.

OK, got that? Phew!

What about friends of friends. That is OK but again as long as they also don't expect mates' rates either (and as long as they are not friends of yours too).

So, there you go! Do not let to friends. End of story.

Chapter 1 - Letting Through a Letting Agent

Well, this is the biggie - letting your property through an estate agent or letting agent.

It is thought that about 50% of all landlords use the services of a high street letting agency to find their next tenants. The bulk of the rest use their own efforts, perhaps also using an "online letting agent". (Don't worry, I will explain the difference between an online and high street letting agent later and how an online agent can help you "do it yourself").

So, which agents do lettings?

Answer: Pretty well all of them, these days.

Sure, there was a time when there were estate agents who only sold houses and did not concern themselves with the mucky business of letting, but these agents are pretty thin on the ground these days. The move to lettings is partly a reflection of market conditions. People now buy and sell houses less often, possibly due to the higher cost of moving, in particular the ever rising cost of Stamp Duty Land Tax. This meant even the most sniffy estate agent now had to do lettings too, whether they liked it or not. So, if you go down most high streets you will find that most estate agents are also in the lettings business.

Now, there is a lot to be said for using a good, professional high street letting agent to find the right tenants for you. But the key words here were *"good, professional letting agents"* and *"right tenants"*.

The trouble is too many high street letting agents are not very good, some are not "professional" and will find you a tenant who is not right for you.

I guess the fact that you have bought this book probably says that you (sort of) understood that fact already and that you are not the kind of person who thinks you can blithely pass on the job of finding a suitable tenant to any old letting agent who happens to come by wearing a shiny suit.

So, we will look at what a high street letting agent actually does, discuss whether they add any value, and if so, how much. We will look at whether using a letting agent is right for you and start to consider whether you are the kind of landlord who could easily find a good tenant yourself and deal with all the admin around it. And if you decide to use a high street letting agent, I'll show you how to find a good one.

Now it must be said right here, right now that we think that even if you've already made up your mind to use a high street letting agent, that you still read the parts of this chapter which looks at the checks that the agent should be doing for you, to ensure they get you a good tenant who will look after the property well, pay the rent on time and not upset the neighbours.

We are not saying you should micro-manage the tenant find process, because if you've elected to use a high street letting agent you've got to trust them to do their job to some extent. However, whilst you must trust them a bit, you cannot just give them carte blanche to run off without any supervision at all. You *must still ensure* they are doing sufficiently robust checks to get a good tenant, especially the first time you use them. That's why I suggest you still read Chapter 2 - which is our *"Do It Yourself"* guide.

High Street v Online Letting Agent

Before we go any further, it's important to understand the difference between high street letting agents and what I'm going to call *"online letting agents"*.

I'm using the term "high street letting agent" to refer to a traditional agent who has a shop or lots of shops somewhere - a physical place you or prospective tenants can walk into. It might be on a high street or it might not be, though most agents opt for some prominent location, often also near a bus stop or train/ tube/ tram station, where they can get a fair bit of passing traffic and visibility. Of course, all high street letting agents will also have their own website on which they will load all their properties available for letting - and in that sense they are also online too.

But when I talk about "online letting agents", I'm really referring to the ones who don't have a presence on the street at all. Sure, they may have an office somewhere, probably on a business park, but *they trade mostly online,* with any optional services they offer, such as the provision of inventories and photographers to take nice pics of your house, being available in an optional "menu" and performed by a network of mostly self-employed workers whom they hire as and when they need them.

So what's the reason for online letting agents? Why do they exist and what landlord need do they fulfil? Well, most basically, they allow landlords a route to getting their properties on the big portals, which is where 95% of tenants look for their next rental.

And landlords in some sectors of the tenant market will be unable to use the services of a high street letting agent anyway.

Many high street letting agents are not keen on doing individual room lets, student lets and housing benefit tenants, so landlords running houses in multi occupation (HMOs) and / or letting to students or people on benefits, often have to find another way to reach their target market. (We will look in more depth at the additional options you have when advertising your property to let to students and / or sharers in HMOs and room lets in Chapter 3).

So for landlords who don't want to use a high street letting agent, they need to find a way to get tenants to see their properties. This means they have to somehow get their properties listed on one or more of the big "portals" who advertise heavily on TV and elsewhere - the main ones being Rightmove, Zoopla and OnTheMarket - which is where the vast majority of tenants looking to rent a property will search. The way they do this is by using the online letting agents (sometimes also called EAgents).

All letting agents - both high street and purely online ones - have to upload all their properties to one or more of the three main portals. They don't really have a choice. The portals spend millions of pounds every year establishing and creating their brands, supporting it through TV ads and all kinds of other marketing initiatives. Everyone has heard of Rightmove, but not everyone is familiar with even the names of even the biggest chains of letting agents such as Savills or Chestertons, much to the chagrin of these agents.

And so the online letting agents offer a solution for private landlords to get their properties marketed. All the landlord needs to do is pay a fee of anywhere from £50 to £100 to the online agent, write some copy, take some pictures and upload their advert to the online letting agent's website. The online agent will then, in turn, upload it to one or more of the portals. In no time at all, the advert is on Rightmove and / or Zoopla and is generating phone and email enquiries from tenants, which are passed on by the online agent and the landlord can follow these up. The landlord can do all the rest of the work himself - the viewings, the tenants' reference checks, arranging gas safety checks etc. - indeed all the work right up to move in date or, if he prefers, he can use some or all of the additional services offered by the online letting agent.

It's probably fair to say that lots of high street agents are not very happy that online agents a) exist at all and b) use the portals in this way. Indeed this has been a bit of a sore point for quite a while, but as long as the online agents pay the portals and the portals (or at least some of them) are happy to continue taking the online agents' money, the online letting agents will continue to feature (and flourish).

Using an online letting agent is a lot cheaper than using a high street letting agent, whose tenant-find fees will start at around 4 weeks' rent plus VAT - and a lot more in London and some other big cities.

Now you might ask, what concern is it of the portals that technology has allowed landlords to take over part of the job of the high street letting agents and effectively perform a lot of the activities themselves? Answer: probably none at all (though, as I said, it has rather upset some letting agents).

Indeed, you could go as far as to say that the likes of Rightmove and Zoopla are just brands associated with buying / selling and letting houses and who have cleverly used the power of advertising and the opportunities afforded by new technology and the internet to change the rules of the property game, and in doing so, changing the role of the traditional agent.

But things are changing all the time. When the new portal, OnTheMarket started in 2014, it did not allow online agents to upload their properties onto it, perhaps not surprising given that OnTheMarket is jointly owned by some fairly blue blooded estate agency chains who had become quite resentful of the charges that the likes of Rightmove and Zoopla levied on agents for marketing properties, let alone the fact that they allowed "pesky" online letting agents to use the portals and compete with the traditional high street letting agent.

So, there's a lot going on - and a lot of competitive manoeuvring in this lettings business.

So where will it all end?

Well, as technology and the way we shop continues to evolve, I think online agents are here to stay. For the landlord who likes to be "hands on" and who is happy to do lots of the letting agency work himself, the online agency concept presents a very cheap way to get exposure on the portals that accept the online agent shilling - thus offering a very big exposure to hundreds of thousands of tenants who each day are looking on the internet to find their next place to live.

Of course, not all landlords want to do all the work that letting agents do. My estimate is that a maximum of 20 to 30 per cent will. The majority will still trust to high street letting agents to do the work around finding tenants - and that is fine.

But for those that like the idea of online letting agents, they remain a very low cost way of getting your property visible, especially when one considers those juicy cost savings. And, here is another thing - the high street agent will also be charging the tenants too, indeed we have seen examples of tenants being charged up to £400 plus £150 per additional tenant in admin fees - which can rightly make tenants feel rather aggrieved from the start - not a good start to a relationship.

Of course, if you are set on carrying out the activities of a letting agent yourself, you will have to spend some time doing it too - and your time may be expensive. If you are not available to do viewings or carry out reference checks quickly, then perhaps you should think again and just go straight to a high street letting agent who will do the whole job for you.

In Chapter 2, we provide a detailed guide to doing it yourself using an online letting agent without using the services of a high street letting agent. If you are convinced this is the way you want to go, then go straight to that chapter. But first, for those who are undecided, we will look at what a high street letting agent does.

What does a High Street Letting Agent Do?

Listed below are the main activities of the *high street letting agent* and comments on the added value of each. This will help you to understand what they do, ask the right questions and ensure you are getting value for your money.

They can tell you the rental potential of your property

Sure, this can be useful, but you could simply look on one of the portals and get a pretty good idea yourself of what rent the place should fetch in five minutes. Just take 5% off to get a competitive rent and off you go. If you price at this level, you should get your place let quickly with no voids. (The ones you are seeing advertised may be overpriced - which is why they are still showing as unlet. It's an obvious paradox that many people "don't get". That's why I say to take off 5%).

Where a decent letting agent should add value is by telling you what you should do to increase the potential rent. This might be something as simple as cleaning the front door, decluttering or making other improvements to increase the potential to help it let faster. They might have useful suggestions on how much furnishing you should provide or whether you should provide any furnishings at all.

They can market the property

Of course they can but you can do this too using an online approach yourself- as we shall see.

A decent agent should be able to produce really good copy that sells the benefits of the home and produce good photographs and floor plans too. (Check out the copy and pictures they have for other properties. If the pictures are poor and the description full of spelling errors or if what they've written fails to sell the benefits, then go elsewhere).

Having a high street presence, they can attract passing trade that might not otherwise be looking online regularly. And of course, they can carry out viewings at times convenient to potential tenants at all times of the day, at times when you might be unavailable.

They can find the right tenants

A good letting agent can find the right tenants - ones that will be right for you and your property. As we've said before, a good tenant is one who will pay the rent on time each and every month, who will look after the property properly and who won't upset the neighbours through antisocial behaviour.

Of course, you have to tell the high street letting agent what kind of tenant you will accept - and you'll need to be very specific about this and put your requirements clearly in writing so the agent is in no doubt.

The letting agent will find the right tenants by carrying out identity, reference, credit and affordability checks on the tenants. There are many parts to this process, which I describe more fully in Chapter 2 (and which you should read) but the main purpose of the checks are threefold.

- To establish whether they are who they say they are - ID and "Right to Rent" checks. (More on Right to Rent later, but checking and keeping copies of ID is now effectively a legal requirement for landlords).

- To establish if they can afford the rent comfortably - Credit and income / affordability checks, including checks with their employer (if they have one)

- To establish past behaviour - What does a past landlord say about them.

I have heard many stories from amateur landlords who got a troublesome tenant through the "good offices" of a letting agent. Far too many! So you simply cannot give the letting agent carte blanche to just go and find any old tenant. This will simply not do. The fact is you must get a bit involved in the process by stating what kind of tenant you want and then making sure that the letting agent has given you the kind of tenant you asked for. Always check to see that the agent completed their checks properly and accurately.

Now, it is worth saying you should not "over-manage" the letting agent, but the agent must understand that you do still have an active interest in what they do for you. A good letting agent will welcome this, providing you are not over-fussy or prevaricating and as long as you are clear about the type of tenant you want right at the outset.

So, I would suggest, as a minimum, you ask the letting agent for sight of copies of the credit reports obtained and retain the final "yes" or "no" decision for borderline applicants.

As mentioned in the previous section, if your target market is individual room lets, perhaps rooms in a house of multi occupation, many high street letting agents will not be interested, fearing (rightly) that workloads in such lets are too high and the returns too low, (which kind of tells you something about such properties and the workload they involve). So, if letting room by room in shared housing is your target market, you may find your friendly high street letting agent will not be able to help you. Some high street letting agents will not take on very low rent properties for the reason that there is not enough money in doing it and others will not want to get involved with student lets or lettings to people who are on housing benefits.

We will look at how to find tenants for these specialist areas in Chapter 3.

They can achieve a premium rent

Whether a high street letting agent can achieve a higher rent than you could acting on your own, perhaps using an online agent, is a debateable point. As people shop ever more online, this premium, if it ever did exist, may start to erode.

Now it is probably true though that there are some tenants who like the comfort that a high street letting agent gives them, especially if that agent will be involved in the management of the let property. Having a physical office to go to where they can complain if things are not being managed right will give some tenants a feeling of comfort. Of course, if the letting agent cannot get hold of the landlord or get the landlord to agree to carry out necessary works, this perceived benefit might not be worth all that much in practice.

But just as there are some tenants who would like a high street letting agent involved in the letting, there are other tenants who are not at all keen - and actually prefer to deal direct with the landlord right from the outset.

Many tenants I have known have told me they have experience of a high street agent "getting in the way"; that messages are not passed onto the landlord and nothing gets done. This may well be true or it might be more the case that the landlord is "hiding behind the agent" and evading his responsibilities to carry out repairs. It is hard to know the true facts in each case.

However, there is one thing that really does bug potential tenants about letting agencies - and that is the fees. Oh yes!

As well as charging the landlord for their services, most high street letting agents also charge tenants' fees too. Of course, landlords operating on their own also often charge fees to tenants, but in most cases they tend to be lower than a high street letting agent.

Fees charged to tenants range over a number of headings - from credit reference checks to inventory fees and more. Many letting agents even make charges for signing the tenancy agreement and for renewing tenancies.

I think the average tenant does not mind paying some fees, but only up to a point and only as long as the fees are reasonable. Most would accept that running credit and previous landlords' and employers' checks does take up some time and does cost some money - which has to be recouped somehow (though some would argue, with some justification, that the rent they are going to pay should more than compensate the landlord and letting agent for this expense).

The average tenant may also rightly ask why they have to pay the high street letting agency a fee when the agent is being paid a "tenant find" fee by the landlord. It's a fair question.

Unreasonably high fees demanded by letting agents from tenants could sour the start of the landlord-tenant relationship even before it has begun. And very high fees levied by letting agents will mean that tenants actually have less money available to pay rent. In such circumstances, a landlord using a high street letting agent may actually end up getting less rent than if he found a tenant under his own steam.

Fees are so unpopular that in 2013 the Scottish Government banned agents and landlords charging fees to tenants for all private lets in Scotland. It looks likely that England, Wales and Northern Ireland could also follow soon, with a ban on at least some forms of fee.

They can save you time

Of course, this is the biggie, this is where a high street letting agent really comes into their own.

Clearly if you are too busy to find and check tenants yourself, a high street letting agent will save you time. Finding tenants is more than just putting an advert up through an online letting agent and then taking the first person who comes through the door.

As we have seen already, it will involve you carrying out checks on the tenants' suitability and ability to pay the rent. It involves making sure the property is ready for occupation - making sure gas checks have been done, that there is an energy performance certificate for the property, the electrics are safe and that smoke and carbon monoxide alarms work. It also involves taking reservation fees, signing tenancy agreements, dealing with guarantors (if applicable), managing the tenants' deposits into one of the approved government schemes, checking the first months' rent is in, recording meter readings and dealing with utility companies and sending them something called the "How to Rent" booklet. (Landlords letting and managing homes in Wales also have to attend a special short training scheme to be licensed with "RentSmart Wales" - and we expect the Scots to follow the Welsh lead soon. And in Scotland and Wales all landlords must go on a register of landlords).

This stuff can be time-consuming work. Even a competitively priced property will take up about 5 man days all told. So, if you don't have the time to do it yourself or your time is too valuable, then of course, the best option is to have a good letting agent take care of it all for you. If you are too far away from the property and don't have anyone local to conduct viewings, you'll have to use a letting agent to show people around. But for goodness sake, be sure the letting agent is good and can be trusted to do all that they need to do and have - contracted to do as a reasonable service for you.

The next section looks at how to choose a good letting agent.

Choosing a good high street letting agent

There are good high street letting agents, there are ones who are bad and there are a lot who are in between. The fact is that anyone with a bit of cash can still set up a letting agency and start trading. Many governments have considered regulating letting agents more, but so far no real action has been taken to significantly raise standards above a basic minimum. So the standards of some are still less than great - and that is being kind.

So let's have a look at the sort of things you need to think about when you come to choose a letting agent.

Start off with finding out what people say about them. Using a search engine look for reviews of local letting agents. Bear in mind that if they are part of chain of letting agents, standards may still vary a lot from branch to branch. Check out what it says online about *that particular branch.* Get a feel for the average review.

What is their office like? Think about its location - will it attract passing trade? What is the office interior like? One thing that you should not see is other people's personal files lying around unsecured on desks or a general cluttered environment.

What are the staff like? Do they give you an impression of professionalism and act as if they care?

What is their record keeping like? Ask them to show you a sample of their current files for both "tenant find" and tenant management. Look to see if the records look tidy and up-to-date and include the information and records that you would expect to see - gas safety records, information on energy performance certificates, tenancy deposit information, inventory information, freeholder information, tenant contact details etc.

What are their adverts like? As noted above, does the copy read well or is it full of bad English and spelling errors. Does it sell the benefits? For example, "Lovely long garden" is not as good as "Super garden for parties and barbecues or just to relax in." How good are the pictures they take? Do they do the property justice? Do the photos help sell it? Are they using historical pictures taken from old files and in a season when the weather would have been very different to what it's like now?

Which portals are they with? Find out which of the property portals they will upload your property to. They should, at least, be on either Rightmove or Zoopla, preferably both, to reach the maximum number of potential tenants.

How fast will they let your property? Ask how long it usually takes. They will likely respond, "Very fast" but don't expect them to give you a guarantee on this! At least it will make them realise they will need to act fast if you hire them.

Ask how they deal with tenants' deposits. Do they protect them and if so, in which scheme? Will they provide you with proof of this? (Generally, if all the letting agent is doing is finding you a tenant, i.e. they are not providing management after that time, I would advise that you look after the protection of the tenants' deposit money yourself. And make sure you don't forget to do this as there are penalties for failing to do it).

What happens when you call out of hours? There should be a facility to record messages and someone should get back to you by Noon the next day.

Ask someone to pose as a tenant and call up whilst you listen in to the call. How professional does the agent sound? Are they good at selling the benefits of the property to potential tenants? What happens when you call up during normal business hours? If no one answers the call, take that as a bad sign.

Do they let properties like yours? This is important because some letting agents tend to specialise in certain types of property, with long-established firms often being particularly keen to corner the "premium" end of the market (and often charging premium prices and fees too). Select an agent who has experience of letting properties like yours and who will therefore be known to tenants as a letting agent who markets properties like yours.

Ask to see a sample of their proposed contract with you. I say "proposed" because you should take the view that no contract is ever set in stone and your job will be to go through it and understand what it is that they will be doing for you and for what price and what they will NOT be doing for you, so you can compare it with what's on offer from other agents. Once you have compared it, you may need to come back with your red pen and suggest amending anything in their contract that you don't like the sound of.

At this stage, your job should be focussed on getting an idea about the services they propose to provide for you and at what approximate cost. You should also ask if there is a minimum term for the contract. I would suggest that for "tenant find" you do not enter into a contract longer than 3 or 4 weeks, because you should want to be able to get out of the contract if they fail to find you a good tenant in that time - and hire a more competent agent.

Ask about their professional history and memberships of umbrella bodies. All letting agents have to belong to an approved ombudsman scheme, which is where you can ultimately complain if things go wrong and their service falls short. But there are a variety of professional bodies that letting agents may belong to as well. However, just because an agent is not a member does not mean they will be useless. Some very good high street agents have a long and distinguished history and provide good service but are not members of certain schemes. Having said that, being a member of one of these does at least give you some additional assurance. The main ones are RICS (the Royal Institution of Chartered Surveyors, UKALA (UK

Association of Letting Agents), NAEA (National Association of Estate Agents), the National Approved Lettings Scheme (NALS) and ARLA (Association of Residential Letting Agents). Membership of these will offer a code of conduct and usually a scheme for client money protection, thus protecting most of your money if the agent should go out of business. In Wales, letting agents must be licensed with RentSmart Wales. See www.RentSmart.gov.wales for more information.

Checking the letting agents contract and negotiating the fee

To some extent the contract and the level of service a high street letting agent provides should be connected to the fee - and both are entirely negotiable. Both may look to be set in stone and printed from a computer, but everything in business can be negotiated. Their fee and service level is no different.

So, how much should you pay and what should you get for this?

Well, it is difficult to be precise because the amounts vary by region and by how easy or difficult the letting agents thinks it will be to let your property - and that will be a function of how it is priced, how much appeal it has to potential tenants, what the level of demand is like currently for that type of property (which can vary through the year), how it's furnished etc. It is beyond the scope of this book to look at these myriad factors. If you want to find more, get hold of my book, *"Successful Property Letting - How to Make Money in Buy to Let."* But as a basic starter, most letting agents price their fees based on a number of weeks' rent.

Outside London, a fair tenant-find fee would be equivalent to about 4 weeks' rent plus VAT. In London, I know of some landlords who pay 6 weeks' plus VAT. Landlords with larger portfolios, especially those with whom agents have established relationships should get fees much lower than even 4 weeks' rent.

So what do you get for this?

Well, for this fee, the letting agent should perform a whole range of activities right through from getting the property advertised on the main portals, to conducting viewings, reference checking tenants, signing agreements, collecting rent and deposits before move in, administering the deposit protection, assisting at check-in by showing them where the boiler/ fuse box is, where instruction manuals / gas safety certificates are, testing the smoke and (if applicable, carbon monoxide) alarms, dealing with the utilities and council tax - and more.

Normally, carrying out an inventory is an additional cost that most agents will charge an extra fee for - and you should absolutely ensure that a thorough professional and independent inventory is done. Don't skimp on this unless you want to give the tenants carte blanche to ruin your property and scupper any chance you have of making a deduction from their deposit.

Of course, any sensible letting agent will try to negotiate with you to do more than just the tenant-find. They will be keen to get you to sign up for them to manage the property throughout the whole of the tenancy. Of course, the fees for doing this are much higher- starting from 8% of the rent plus VAT, with many managing to get as much as 15% of the rent plus VAT. However, I know of experienced landlords with much larger portfolios, which are all managed by the same agent, who have achieved as low as 3% to 5% plus VAT.

Whether you take up their offer to fully manage is again dependent on how much time you have available to deal with tenant and property issues, as and when they arise. Again, there are many considerations here that are beyond the scope of this book. Read my book, *"Successful Property Letting"* for more on this.

Whatever you decide to do, bear in mind that whilst any decent high street letting agent will have people on their books who can fix boilers, plumbing, roofs, gutters, electrics and more besides, the letting agent will also likely load up another fee for doing any such works before they bill you for the works. This will be in addition to what you pay them for managing the property.

I reckon that 80% of maintenance /call out jobs from tenants are for boilers, plumbing and drains issues. These can all be fixed by a competent gas engineer providing he can also do plumbing (and many can). Roofs and gutters and other leaking stuff accounts for about 5% of work and electric related stuff another 5%. So, if you have access to or know good tradesmen who can do these jobs promptly when you need them doing, do you really need a letting agent to manage the property for you? You must decide for yourself.

But whatever you do, if you use an agent for the tenant-find work only, I would strongly suggest that you check the letting agents' agreement and strike out any clause that may require you to pay them another round of fees every time the tenant renews the tenancy. This is money for old rope and you should challenge it.

My suggestion is, if you have not hired the agent for full management, then you should only pay the agent a one off tenant-find and move-in fee, at which point your contractual relationship should end. After all, at the end of the initial fixed period of the tenancy, if you want it to continue, a brief email or letter from you stating this to the tenants is all that is needed. At this point the tenancy becomes what is called a "monthly periodic tenancy" and it runs from month to month, for as long as you and the tenants want it to continue. This requires no special forms, just a letter or email from you and the tenants' agreement to it. Job done and surely not worth paying a letting agent a fortune to do this, is it?

Finally, you need to be clear what the word "agency" means. When you hire someone to act as your agent and sign an agreement to that effect, you are bound by agreements or contracts made by that agent on your behalf with a third party, whether a tenant or a supplier. If the agent agrees to do something which you have not authorised, you are still bound by that agent's actions, unless it is a thing which is obviously outside the authority of a normal agent. And if he goes bust taking the tenants deposit with him and it turns out he did not protect it, you will still be liable for the return of the deposit to the tenant. (This is why it's important to check the agency has client money protection cover).

So be clear about what the limits of the agent's authority are. Read their proposed contract with you and amend anything you don't like. And keep a copy. If they break the instructions you gave them - say they let a property to someone with a dog, when you put in writing, "No Pets", they will be liable to you for losses which follow from this.

Chapter 2 - Finding Tenants Yourself

As explained before, the great thing about technology change is that it has newly afforded lots of landlords the power to effectively become their own letting agent without having to pay high street letting agency fees - and you can do this using what we call an "online" or E-Letting agent.

Of course, it might happen that at some point the big portals could restrict their use to pure high street letting agents only, as the portal OnTheMarket has already done. But I think this is unlikely - competition and the changing nature of the way products and services are marketed, (and letting property is no different), means there will always be a choice of portals which are open to landlords to use to market properties direct to tenants.

Why do the job of finding a tenant yourself? Why cut out the high street letting agent?

Well, it puts you in control and it's not that hard to do, providing you have a little time to do it. It will save you money too - with fees ranging from as low as £50 to around £100 to place an advert to let a property for as long as you like.

But before we go on, let's pause for a moment and look at the objective, which is to get a good tenant who will look after your property and pay rent on time, every time and not upset the neighbours. And to get them quickly so that the property does not sit empty costing you money.

Sounds simple doesn't it - and in many ways it is.

However, there is some stuff you need to know. This section will explain everything you need to understand so you can do it yourself.

So, let's break down the business of finding a tenant into its component parts.

The first step is to market your property, to get it out there so people can see that you actually have a property to let.

The second step is to choose a suitable tenant from among the responders to your marketing efforts. This will involve ensuring that the process from someone saying they will take it to them actually paying you and then moving in is as smooth as possible. We call this the "Screening-to-Move In" process.

The second step is longer than the first. Both must be done carefully and with care and attention to detail. I'm going to explain everything.

Step One - Marketing Your Property

There are a number of ways to go about marketing your property and to some extent how you go about it will depend upon what sort of property you have and the tenant market you are aiming at.

A tried and tested way to reach the largest number of tenants for any property is to get your property on line at one of the main portals. And the largest portals that currently accept adverts from online letting agents are Rightmove and Zoopla.

Getting your place advertised on there too is simple. You use one of any one of a number of different online letting agents who will upload to most of the main portals - and off you go. This approach will work for most tenant markets, but there are a few "special situations" which might call for a different marketing approach to be used either instead of or, more usually, in addition to, using an online letting agent.

There are really just a few special situations.

1 Upmarket properties. Some upmarket properties in very upmarket parts of London, Surrey, Manchester and Edinburgh might also benefit from being marketed by relocation agents and specialist upmarket estates agencies. These agencies will generally also use the main portals - but it is worth contacting relocation agents directly. Simply plug in your area, e.g. "London + relocation agents" into your search engine and contact a few, to see if they can help you.

2 Students. If you are planning to let to students, other marketing approaches using word of mouth, local contacts, the university or college accommodation office itself and specialist websites might be useful and worth considering. I will look at this more in Chapter 3.

3 If you are just letting on a room by room basis there are a number of specialist websites that will also reap dividends for you. Again, I will look at this in Chapter 3.

But the main approach will be to use an online letting agent, so let's look in real detail at how to market your property using an online agent.

The first thing to do is to write some copy and take some pictures of the property you have to let. And this sounds easy - surely anyone can dash out some words and take a few snaps. Well, yes they can, and you can too, and it will get you started. But if you do that you may be wasting a lot of opportunities, minimising the numbers of potential tenants who will enquire with you and it could actually lead to you wasting a lot of your valuable time.

I would suggest that you spend a little bit of time looking at the other adverts on Rightmove and Zoopla. See which ones appeal to you, which ones really sell the benefits of the properties being marketed?

We want to maximise our responses - this is what all good marketeers of any product or service do. So, think about it carefully and first write some good words that really sell the *benefits* of your property to your target tenant group.

You should certainly aim to specify the layout of the home, to almost "talk" the potential clients through it. Say what's on each floor (if there is more than one) and what happens when you open the front door, for example, "The front door opens onto the hall, with ample space for coats and storage and then from there into a spacious reception room...."

Give room sizes of each room - in meters and in feet too - and make it clear if the room leads off another room or whether the room leads off a hall.

And don't forget to mention the garden (including dimensions) and any parking spaces as well - and if there is parking, state if there are any parking charges and whether a parking space is allocated for the property specifically or shared with others on a first-come first served basis.

If it is in a quiet road, then say this - and if it is in a cul-de-sac, then say this too, as lots of people will prefer this as there will be less traffic noise and if they have children, playing outside will be safer.

Always refer to the property as a *home*, not as a "house" or "flat". It will be the tenants home and the word home conveys more positive images than "property" or "flat", though you might also use the word "apartment" which somehow sounds a bit more upmarket.

However, don't overindulge on the hyperbole or be tempted to be over flowery in your description of the property, sorry, home! Just keep to the description and sell the benefits gently, but don't oversell. For example, "The south facing garden gets lots of sunshine and is an ideal spot for a barbecue at most times of year" is just fine. (And note, on the subject of sun, if the whole property is light and bright and if it faces south or west, mention that too. People do not like to live in a gloomy environment.)

It is worth stating something about the local area, again in terms of benefits - e.g. close to shops, a short walk to the station, adjacent to a lovely park, in the catchment area for three great schools etc. And mention the local bus and train services: "Buses 321 and 55 get you to the heart of Leeds in under 10 minutes."

If local council tax is low then say so. This is especially relevant in London where council tax can vary a great deal between boroughs. (Go on line and compare local council tax rates - they vary more than you might think).

It is also worth saying if the property is well insulated and warm, for example: "The home benefits from gas central heating from a modern, recently installed condensing boiler and double glazing and the south facing aspect is good for keeping heating bills down." This all helps sell the benefits of low bills and warmth, which can be particularly relevant if you are marketing the property in the depths of winter. Hopefully, folks who are fed up of living somewhere that's cold and damp will rush to see it! Of course, applicants can always read the energy performance certificate, which must, by law, be shown on all adverts for let properties, but it does no harm to restate the benefits of low heating bills in your advert copy too.

Headline bullet points are also useful to "sell" the main benefits. The online letting agency UPAD recommend you do this - and it is good practice. So try to think of the three or four things that you think will most appeal about your property and put them at the start of your advert. It might be:

- Superb, spacious two double-bedroom home in the heart of Bristol
- Quiet road, near to sought after St Thomas's school
- Newly decorated to a high standard for comfortable living

Hopefully, this kind of copy will generate a lot of interest, which is great. But you may not want to show the property to everyone who enquires because not all of them will be the type of applicants whom you want as tenants.

Deciding the type of applicants you want as tenants is beyond the scope of this book - but it's an exercise you must go through before you start marketing your property, indeed, ideally before you even buy a property with a view to letting it. Obviously, the type of applicant you get will be influenced by where the property is, how upmarket it is and a range of other factors dictated by what your research has told you is the size and attractiveness of the relevant tenant markets.

Your advert copy should make this clear because you really don't want to waste time getting enquiries from people for whom the property is not at all suitable.

If you don't want students, say so in the copy. If you don't accept housing benefit tenants say that too. I usually put in the advert something like, "Proof of ID and sufficient funds to pay the rent will be required. A deposit will be required equivalent to 6 weeks' rent. Deposits will be protected in an approved tenancy deposit scheme". If you only want working tenants you could instead put, "Proof of income sufficient to pay the rent will be required" rather than the more amorphous "sufficient funds will be required."

Of course, it goes without saying that your advert and your processes should not discriminate on grounds of sex, sexual orientation, race, religion or disability. If you do this, you should rightly feel the effects of the law.

If the property is being let unfurnished or only with "white goods" (fridge-freezer, cooker and washing machine) then state that too. That does not mean the photos you use in your advert should show it unfurnished. I think the photos you use should absolutely show it furnished, (providing of course, the property looks good furnished) as this will give applicants the idea of what it will look like as a home. Indeed, many professional landlords will "dress" a property for letting, or at least for photographs so that it looks in the best light. Then, once the property is let, they move all the furnishings out ready for the next property they have available to let.

If you charge tenants for reference checking or you make any other charges, (other than rents and deposit payments), it is a legal requirement that you state what these are and what they are for, but try and be brief about this as you don't want to detract too much from selling the benefits of the home itself. (Note: If your property is in Scotland you cannot charge fees and the other countries of the UK may follow suit).

It is a legal requirement that there must be an Energy Performance Certificate (EPC) for the property and this must be less than ten years old. The online letting agent should be able to link up to this as the document should be publicly available. If you don't have one, the online letting agent will probably not accept the listing for your property until you've had one done.

Don't worry. EPCs are not expensive. They cost from around £80 for a two bed property. The bigger the property the bigger the cost. Search online for a cheap quote from a Domestic Energy Assessor and if the energy efficiency of the property has been improved since the last one was done - e.g. if you had a new boiler - then get a new one done, as a good score for energy efficiency will help you let it.

They say every picture tells a story - and that is true of advertisements too. The words you write are all good, but you really must have some good pictures to show the place off to its full potential.

If the pictures show the property furnished, your advert copy must state clearly that it is going to be let unfurnished or part-furnished with just white goods, (if that is what you intend to do).

Pictures that show an unmade bed with clothes and pizza wrappers all over the floor and a stack of unwashed dishes in the sink just won't cut it and will severely reduce your advert's response rate. Prospective tenants will take one look and think, "Well, if the landlord cannot even be bothered to show his property at its best, as a home, what kind of landlord will he be?" And they will be right.

So, take time to take good pictures that show the property in its best light. Think about lighting and use the best angles that present the property in the best way possible. Think too about the order of the photos that take the prospective tenants through the front door into the home in a logical order. This should match up with the copy order, as far as possible. However, if there is one room that is particularly good, you might want to present that as the first picture. Generally, though, it is best to have an outside picture first - so tidy up outside ready for the picture - and keep it tidy for the viewings too as first impressions, sometimes called "kerb appeal" are paramount. And if you are really hopeless at taking a good quality photo, then consider hiring a professional to take some for you. (Some online letting agents will provide one for a fee). Keep the best photos on a file to use next time.

The Screening-to-Move in Process

Selection of Tenants - The Initial Screening Process

Unfortunately, the nature of this business means that there will be many people applying who will be completely unsuitable as tenants. They won't have read your advert properly and they won't have read what kind of tenants you don't want, so they will call or email, thus wasting their own time as well as yours. So, you'll have to be ready to pre-screen callers who don't fit your spec.

The best way to screen tenants is by phone, rather than email - as this gives you more chance to ask questions. Have a notebook ready to jot down their responses and any other things they tell you.

But before you really let them say too much, you have to take control of the conversation. The initial conversation will usually involve them saying, "Hi, we saw your advert on Acme

Lettings Website / Rightmove and we would like to see the property. Is it still available?"

Your response is "Hi Mrs. X, yes it is still available and we would love to show you the property, but we just need to ask a few questions first to ensure the property is suitable for you."

What questions you ask next will depend on the type of tenants you want to let to. Generally, my properties are only available to tenants who won't need to rely on housing benefit to pay the rent. But it might be that you accept students and / or people who are on housing benefit, in which case your questions will be different. If you accept these groups, read on to the end of this section, but afterwards please refer also to Chapter 3, which deals with the slight differences that apply for those particular tenant types.

The next thing we say is, "The property is available from X date and the rent is £X per month plus a £Y deposit. Is that OK?" Then we say, "Who is the property for?"

This last question can produce a long rambling answer sometimes, so you have to be able to butt in, if you need to and if necessary, though don't be too quick, as what they say in response to this can produce very valuable information that you should jot down. So, let them speak.

The reason for asking this sort of fairly open question is because the answer will tell you what kind of tenant group this is. Is it a family? Is it sharers? Who are they? (Of course, if you prefer a certain type of tenant group - say a couple or a family for instance and not sharers, your advert should state this, (though it will reduce your market a bit, so think carefully before you do this)). Generally family groups and couples tend to stay longer than groups of sharers, so that might influence your thinking.

The next question you need to ask is about their work and their income. This is how I phrase it, "Obviously we need to know that you can afford the rent comfortably. So may I ask what your approximate combined incomes are please? There is no point bothering to show a property to someone who will struggle each month to pay the rent.

A logical follow-on question is, "What do you do for a living?" although they may well already have volunteered that information earlier. Indeed, you want the applicants to be coming forward with information as much as possible as any vagueness may possibly indicate a lack of financial means to pay the rent.

The final question is, "Where are you living now?" This is a purposely vague and open ended question. It could mean where - as in location - or instead, it can mean in what sort of accommodation. This is the chance for them to tell you whether they own their own home, if they are living with parents or if they are renting from a landlord or letting agent. And they may also volunteer information about why they are leaving the place they are in now, which is always good to know - so, if they do, jot it down. It is all useful information that can be verified later.

If they don't tell what their current living circumstances are, you must ask, especially if you feel that any of the answers they have given already sound a little evasive.

All the questions should be asked with politeness and tact. You are not conducting the Spanish Inquisition here but you *do* have a right to ask the questions, because you don't want to waste their time or yours showing them a property when they don't have a cat in hells chance of meeting your criteria.

So, what kind of things would make you reject them at this stage?

Well, assuming you are looking for working tenants who are not benefit dependent and not students, you really will need them to have a combined income of at least 2.25 times the rent. Anything less, and they may struggle- which is not good news at all, especially when I tell you that when people don't pay the rent, you normally cannot even start an action to recover the property until they have missed two months' rent payments. Even then, the slow and cumbersome court processes will mean that it will be at least another three months until they have actually gone - making at least five months of lost rent in total (which you will often have little chance of ever recovering through debt collection procedures if they are broke).

If your checks show they are not UK citizens and their home country is outside of the European Economic Area (which means the European Union plus the states of Iceland, Switzerland, Norway and Lichtenstein) then you must ask if they have a work permit and a "right to rent" in the UK. If they don't have a right to legally be in the UK and / or to work here (and risk getting kicked out by the Border Force) then you will not be able to let your property to them. Indeed you'd be breaking the law if you did. Details on what checks you need to do are available at this link: **https://www.gov.uk/check-tenant-right-to-rent-documents/who-to-check** (Following the UK's decision to leave the EU, whether EEA citizens will in future need to prove a "right to rent" remains to be seen and will depend on what precise deal the UK negotiates).

You should remind them if the property is unfurnished and remind them of the earliest date the property becomes available to move into. Obviously, you will have put this information in the advert copy, but as I said before, you cannot expect everyone to have read the ad carefully.

Finally, you should tell them that you will require to see proof of income, ability to afford the rent and proof of ID as well as current work and previous landlord references. And then leave a pause to see what they say.

They may ask you more about what proofs you need and what form the references should take - and if they do, that is a good sign, so be ready to tell them. I'll explain more about what things we actually need to see in the following sections.

Final Steps before the Viewing... And Why We Send a "Confirming Email"

At this stage, if the initial conversation has gone OK, and you like what you hear from the applicants over the phone, then you can arrange a viewing.

We suggest you follow up with an email setting out exactly what you will ultimately need in terms of references / proof of income/ ID checks along with more information on the property and the area, timescales, details of what the rent payment is, how much the deposit is and by when you will need them to pay a reservation fee.

This sounds like a lot of information to send, but they will have been calling a lot of places, making a lot of email enquiries, so reminding them in writing all about the property and what you will want from them, is helpful and it also means they have the answers to most of their questions before they even get to the property, so they can concentrate on the property itself.

Another good reason for sending a full package of information by email is that it helps to deal with those people who may not have been exactly honest during the initial phone call enquiry or who perhaps were covering up something and those who just cannot seem to say "No". The fact is that there are many people who don't like saying "No". Some people just hate to say, "Sorry, this property is not for me" or "Sorry, but I really don't earn enough to qualify for it" or "Sorry, I need to move into a property next week and you've just told me it's not available until August."

I actually think inability to say "No" is a cultural thing. Possibly, this is less of a problem for Americans - they seem the best at straight talking, but there are many other cultures around the world where saying "No" is not in their culture either. British people are sort of in the middle when it comes to this!

Knowing this, we have learnt that sending an email to the applicants can also sort out those people who don't want to say "No" but who will just not turn up to the viewings - and these people are the real timewasters. It also helps weed out those who have not been exactly straight, because when they see it in writing that we intend to conduct a proper reference check as well as checks on ID and their ability to pay, they will effectively withdraw themselves from the process.

Before I close the phone call, this is what I say, "OK, it sounds like the property might be right for you and you might be the kind of tenant we want. I have provisionally booked an appointment for you to view the property at 630pm tomorrow. What I am going to do now is send you an email which will confirm everything about the property that you will need to know. It has information about the property itself, a list of furnishings that are provided at the property and some information about the area, together with some useful links about the area. The email also lists what references we will need from you and what proofs of income and ID we need from you too, should you decide you want to go ahead. It explains what our fees are for conducting these checks. And finally, it sets out what happens once we have completed reference checks and in the run up to move in date as well as some more information on what you need to do on the move in date and shortly afterwards. Please read this email carefully. Once you have read it, we'll need you to call us or email us to reconfirm the appointment. If we don't hear from you, we will assume you don't want to keep the viewing and we will give the viewing slot to someone else. Please do tell us if you find you cannot make that viewing slot and you need to reschedule."

Phew! Ok, that's a longish statement, but we find it works well. And as you can see, we have put the onus on the applicants to read the email and to confirm the appointment. The email and the attachment that goes with it does contain a lot of information - and you might think that it's best not to bother. You might think, "All this information risks just putting them off so let's just get them round to see the property".

Well, when you've had experience of many timewasters who cannot seem to say "No" and who fail to turn up for an appointment on a wet Monday evening that you've driven for 30 minutes to get to, you'll start to appreciate why we send the email.

So what is in the confirming email? Well, as much as you like really. Mine runs to just over four pages with the bulk of the information in an attachment.

The covering email text simply restates what we just said verbally on the phone. It thanks them for their interest, states the viewing appointment time and asks them to read the attachment carefully as it contains important information. The text stresses that once they have read the attached file and if they are happy to proceed, they will need to call you or email you back to reconfirm the viewing appointment. It reiterates that if you don't hear back from them with their confirmation within an hour or two, the appointment will be cancelled and the slot given to another applicant. However, they are free to set up an appointment for another time.

Let's have a look at what is in the attachment that goes with this email.

The first section is about all about the property, the area and the tenancy contract basics. It starts off with a brief summary of the property including the full address with postcode and links to the entry pages of the property at Rightmove or Zoopla, a map of the road on Google Maps and any other links that might prove useful, especially bus routes and links from the internet about why the area is a great place to live in. If the property is hard to find it is a good idea to provide directions on how to find it easily.

I include information on the council tax band it is in and the name of the current utility suppliers. I state what is in the property in the way of furnishings. You may also want to add a statement that you are unable to add or remove furnishings. (This is, of course, up to you and will depend on your level of flexibility and whether you have storage space to store any stuff incoming tenants may not need).

I restate the level of rent in pounds per calendar month. (I suggest all adverts should express the rent in £s per calendar month not per week). I state the level of tenancy deposit that will be required and which approved scheme will be used to protect the deposit. I insert the current link to the "How to Rent" government guide, which contains useful guidance for the tenant. (It is now a legal requirement that tenants are given this, though you should also include a hard copy of it with your tenancy agreement too).

It is normal in most tenancies (apart from some HMOs and lodger situations) that the tenant has to pay for council tax, electricity and gas, water, TV licence. It is worth stating this too, in case anyone is in any doubt. I also add that they are liable to pay all charges in respect of the installation, setting up of and the connection of any phone, TV or broadband installation and line too. It is strongly recommended that they also take out their own contents insurance, and that this includes Accidental Damage Cover to protect them in the case of accidental breakages / damage.

I restate when the property is available from and add a rider that this date may vary by a few days. If it is possible that the property may be available earlier than this date, if the current tenants move out earlier, then this is worth saying too. There is also information on what form of contract the tenancy agreement will take. Normally it will be an assured shorthold tenancy. Unless you are letting a room in your home, we suggest you go for this option as it is safest and also that you set an initial six month term, extendable (if you both agree), once the term has ended (and if all has gone well and you both wish it to continue, of course). Six months seems short but you can always extend it - and it protects you if things don't work out. (It is quicker to regain possession this way, trust me).

It is probably worth adding that, should the tenancy continue on after the end of the initial fixed term, the rent will be adjusted on a regular basis. Most landlords opt for an adjustment every 12 months.

I also add, "We will always look to extend the tenancy after the end of the fixed term as long as everything has gone well". Providing this is your intention, of course, it makes sense to say this now as most tenants will hopefully be looking to make the place their home for a longer term than just six months. And given the costs associated with re-letting and the risks of there being a void period (when the property is empty), you ought to be interested in a longer term relationship than just six months too.

Finally, I state, "Where there is to be more than one tenant, all tenants are jointly, severally and individually liable for the whole rent under a single contract". This is a very important point to make, especially to any applicants who are not spouses or in a partnership, whether legal or otherwise. This statement simply makes it clear that if there is more than one person on the tenancy agreement, each person is liable for the *whole rent*. And for this reason, and in case of any doubt, I also say that I prefer the payment of rent to be made in full by a single bank transfer payment each month.

You could, of course, send them a blank copy of a sample tenancy agreement of the type that you will be using, but I think this is overkill at this stage, as these usually run to well in excess of twelve pages. (We do send them on request, if prospective tenants ask for them).

Next, I include some information on our fees and when they need to be paid. It is now a legal requirement to state what your fees are. (Note, remember, if you are letting property in Scotland, you are not allowed to charge any fees at all, though a refundable reservation fee is normally acceptable, once all reference and other checks have been carried out and completed and a formal offer has been made).

I include information on the references and documentation I need to see as part of the assessment process. This is quite specific as you will see.

Finally, I list all the steps leading up to move in date and after the move in date.

Taken together, the document they are sent contains all the information the tenants will need to know if they are going to let the property from you - and the process they will need to follow to secure that property.

In the appendix at the end of the book, to save you trouble of making up your own, I provide the template for the attachment I use. You might like to make up your own version based on this. I call the document "About the Property and the Contract". Have a read of it - very carefully. Every word is there for a reason. Once you have read it, read on to the next section about reference checks and the steps up to move in.

Finally, if the annual rent happens to be over £100,000 per annum and / or the tenant entity is a company and not an individual, the form of contract will not be an assured shorthold tenancy, but the contract between you and the tenant will be governed by contract law instead. One small advantage of this is that you don't have to protect the deposit in a tenancy deposit scheme.

It's worth noting that in Scotland, an imminent change to the law is expected to prevent landlords from, in future, being able to recover possession of a property unless a tenant has breached the tenancy in such a way that a court awards the landlord possession. In other words, it will effectively abolish what's known as the "no fault ground" or Section 21 ground. Also, Scotland and Wales may also introduce their own forms of tenancy agreement.

About the References and Steps to Move in Date

As you can see, there is a lot of information that goes in this attachment to our email. Potentially a lot to read, yes, but we have found it does cut out the timewasters.

One thing you might notice is that we ask the applicants to get hold of the references that we want to see, rather than us seeking them out. This is a part of the application process that we have effectively "reverse engineered".

Most High Street letting agents operate in the old way. What happens with a high street agent, is a tenant who is interested in a property will typically fill in an application form at the agent's office. The agent will ask for proof of identity and proof of address (most will just ask for a utility bill to prove this). They will also ask for three years' worth of addresses, just as we do. But here the similarity ends. The High Street agent will then send all this information off to a separate credit and reference checking agent who will run a credit check on each tenant as well as contact their current employer and any previous landlord referees.

As you can see from the process described in our document, we put the onus *on the tenants* to get the employer and landlord references and we run the credit check ourselves. Also, we ask *the tenants* to get their three months' of bank statements as an extra proof (or not) as to their ability to rent the property comfortably.

I think this is a better way of doing things. For a start, it puts the onus on the tenant to get the information from employers and landlords that we need to see. This makes far more sense because hopefully the tenant is motivated to get it and will get it much faster. (As you can see from the document we send, they are told we cannot "hold" a property pending receipt of suitable references and proof of ID and address). This makes them very motivated to get the references back quickly.

Consider the alternative with a High Street letting agent. What happens there?

Well, the high street letting agent will pass the tenants' application onto whichever company does their credit checks - and there may be some delay whilst this handover happens. Then the reference checking company sends a request to the employer and previous landlords. Is responding to the reference request going to be a priority for the personnel department in the company? Hardly! Does the reference checking company asking for the references care if they come back fast? Again, hardly - they have never met you nor the tenant, so why would they care as much as you?

With the way we do it, you can bet your bottom dollar that the tenant applicant has a very strong interest in getting his or her employer and previous landlords to write the references we need to see. It works too as we tend to find that the references are usually with us within 24 hours. And of course, the tenant applicants can immediately give us sight of their last three months' bank statements. With their permission, we run a credit check anyway, as a back-useful up, but simply being able to see the last set of bank statements is very useful as it will quickly reveal if the applicant is in a decent financial position as it shows all their income and outgoings.

The cost of running a simple credit check is about £10 to 15 per applicant, depending on which agency you use - and the response is instantaneous. (We use the facility offered by the National Landlords Association, which comes priced at a discount to members, but there are many other service providers - just search online). To be able to perform the credit check you need the full name and date of birth for each applicant and their UK addresses for each of the last three years, together with the dates they lived at each address. The addresses should be the ones they generally use for financial correspondence (e.g. credit card, banking, mobile phone bills, where they are listed on the voters' roll etc.)

Apart from the ID check, probably the main documents we use in our assessment is the applicants' bank statements combined with the credit report check. The bank statements can usually prove their address as well as showing they are "good for the money" and that their income is enough and is also reliable and reasonably constant. (For self-employed people, whose incomes may be more variable, we always ask for six months' bank statements). If the bank statement shows their address, then you will not need to see a separate utility bill proving this. If it doesn't, then get three months' worth of utility or mobile phone bills as well.

The credit check should simply back up the bank statement information, confirm if they are "found" at the addresses given as well as telling you if they have any "nasties" on their file, such as a county court judgement.

Some applicants struggle to get their landlord and employer references back quickly, so we always suggest they put in a request for these as soon as possible and that they chase them up too.

Employers can be particularly tardy with turning around reference requests. However, you can often see from website searches that the individual does indeed work at the company concerned. Alternatively, you could try calling them at their place of work via the main switchboard. If the switchboard operator says they don't work there, take that as a bad sign!

Finally, you could ask to see payslips to verify proof of income (though the fact that money is coming in should also be clear from their bank statements). If they have only just started (or are about to start) a new job, sight of a contract of employment may suffice instead of an employer reference, providing everything else stacks up and looks genuine.

Previous and current landlord references are probably the weakest reference source document and many applicants struggle to get them at all. This can be because their landlord is not contactable or because the relationship has broken down.

You'll recall that in the very first contact we always ask why they are leaving their current place and what their current landlord is like. If they previously told you they are leaving because their landlord is of the idiot variety (yes they do exist!) and he has not fixed the boiler for two months, then he is not going to be the type of person who is going to get off his a*** for a minute and write a reference.

Of course, the applicant tenant may be able to get a reference from an earlier landlord, but most don't keep records of past landlords' names and contact details, so this may also draw a blank.

Landlord references can be faked - and you have to be alive to this possibility. If you get a reference from their current landlord, you can check whether that person really does own the property at the UK land registry. This costs just £3 and takes a few minutes. But even then, there can be "validation problems". In a few cases we found the names did not match but, on investigation, we found that the person the applicant was formerly paying their rent to were actually subletting from the real owner. All the other documents the applicant provided "stacked up" and it was clear that the tenant was innocent of the sublet situation. We let the property to the tenant and they turned out to be just fine. (Land Registry data can be up to 6 months behind too - relevant if the property in question has recently been bought or sold).

Tenants who formerly lived at home with their parents or in college accommodation, are coming from overseas or have moved from their owned property will not have a reference from a current UK landlord.

To conclude, you have to look at all the references and documents you have got and ask yourself if it all looks right and does it "stack up" as a whole picture. Over time, you'll get better at assessing applicants. However, in your early days, if you have any major doubts about someone's suitability or if there is something that does "just not feel right" you should walk away and decline to let to them.

Apart from their references and the suite of documents, there are some other tell-tale signs of someone who will turn out to be a troublesome tenant and general pain in the backside.

Anyone who turns up very late with no attempt at an apology should be rejected outright. Anyone who calls you five times en route for directions should be rejected too. (If they can't be organised to get a map what will they be like as tenants?). Anyone who turns up in a filthy vehicle with old fag wrappers and assorted rubbish on the dashboard will probably treat your property the same way. Give them a wide birth. (And yes, if you can, find an excuse to see their vehicle at the viewing).

Keep copies of all references, ID documents and permits to work in the UK (if applicable) on file as long as the tenancy lasts. After that time, they should be destroyed.

One last point, you will see that we ask for a three week reservation fee initially. There is nothing to stop you asking for the whole first months' rent and deposit, (i.e. all the money), as soon as all the reference checks are cleared. I suggest you do this if the property is vacant, if the move in date is very close or if the applicant offers it.

The only reason I ask for the reservation fee only is because I'm a nice guy and I know it may help the applicant with cash flow whilst they are moving. You don't have to be as nice as me!

One thing to be wary of is people who offer to pay the whole six or 12 months' rent up front. This may sound tempting but you must still do all the relevant checks described here. (Folks setting up cannabis farms often use this approach to get access to a property, so you must be particularly on your guard).

Of course, there is more to being a landlord than just sticking an advert up and finding tenants. There are a number of other regulations that you have to comply with, even before you have found a tenant and then afterwards as well, once they have moved in. The full details are beyond the scope of this book, but you would be advised to check out my book, *"Successful Property Letting - How to Make Money in Buy to Let"* if you want to understand your full responsibilities as a landlord and to ensure you buy the right type of property that will let fast and go up in value - both in terms of rent achieved and value of the property itself.

Chapter 3 - The Special Situations - Letting to Students, Letting Room by Room, Lettings to Housing Benefit Dependent Tenants and Guaranteed Rent Long Lease Schemes

In this chapter I look at the "special renting situations" that these days are perhaps not that "special" or "unusual" at all.

In recent years there has been an increasing tendency for people to rent a house or flat together with other people to whom they are not related. To some extent this is a reflection of the lack of housing and also of changing ideas about communal living. House sharing has been a common thing among students for years, but is increasingly the norm for young professionals too.

At the same time we are seeing more and more people dependent on universal credit / housing benefit to pay some or all of their rent.

There are additional ways of reaching both sorts of tenants and approaches you should use, in conjunction with the approach I set out in Chapter 2.

Letting to House Sharers (Including Students)

In the student sharing markets, timing the market matters more than in other markets.

In many college and university towns, the students will be out trying to secure accommodation in private rented houses long before the new student year starts (the university year generally commences in October and the further education college year starts in September). In many towns and cities, a busy period will be January and February when current students will be starting to think about and trying to secure accommodation for the following year. There may be another busy period in late August and September as they scramble to secure accommodation at the last minute.

Often, securing accommodation for the new student year may be more a case of asking around among older students who are leaving at the end of the year as well as checking the student accommodation office. So, as an existing landlord in this market, you may find that the next years' batch of tenants finds you rather than you having to find them. This will save on marketing cost and your time.

Some college accommodation offices are better than others and the good ones will have lists of landlords, who may also need to be accredited with the accommodation office in order to be listed. So, get in with them and see what you have to do, to be listed.

However, students will not overlook traditional letting agents and portals like Rightmove, so the type of marketing we described in Chapter 2, using an online or high street letting agent, should not be discounted. (However, some high street letting agents will not let to students, seeing it as too much hassle).

Many professional sharers, as well as students, also use specialist house sharing websites like SpareRoom and EasyRoomMate and for students there are specialist sites like AccommodationForStudents. These specialist sites are often free for the basic service and even the higher grade service is usually cheaper than the costs of using other online letting agents. However, they do not all currently upload to the likes of Rightmove and the other big portals, so their reach is limited. Nevertheless, many landlords find they can easily fill individual rooms and/ or student lets using such websites and without ever needing to get their places on Rightmove or Zoopla.

Renting a Shared House - HMOs and the rules on Licensing and Health and Safety

Special rules and regulations apply to letting a house or flat in multiple occupancy, (often called an "HMO") which is defined as a home where three or more people occupy it but don't form a single "household" i.e. because at least two of the people are not related. There are special rules for the management of these properties and depending where the property is and / or how big it is, you may need to get a special license from the local council.(If you are buying with a mortgage, you'll also need the right type of mortgage financing, buying an HMO with a simple buy to let mortgages may not be allowed).

HMO licenses usually last for a five year term and it can cost up to £1500 to get a license for each property, though the fee varies greatly across different councils.

Also, in some areas under what's known as "Article 4" rules, many local authorities now require owners to seek planning permission if they want to turn their property into a house of multiple occupation (HMO).

A key consideration is whether to let under just a single tenancy for the whole property, which each tenant signs with all jointly and severally responsible for paying the rent or to let using different tenancy agreements *for each of the rooms in the property*, with each tenancy agreement defining the room to be let and the communal areas.

In the latter situation, the tenants will have exclusive occupation of their designated room and share the use and facilities of the house or flat (e.g. bathroom, toilet, kitchen and sitting room) with other occupiers of the property.

There are pros and cons of each approach. Letting by the room will require more input from you as people come and go, but letting a whole large house to a group of sharers may result in longer periods where the property is empty (because there may not be that many large groups of friends around).

Whichever route you take, be clear in your marketing about what bills are included and excluded from the rent. In some house shares, you may opt to pay for some of the utilities - water, heating, TV / broadband and council tax, though if students are entirely in occupation, there should, at least, be no council tax for them to pay, as full-time students are exempt. The council will want proof that they are students.

Generally, in order to control costs, I advise to put all the other bills in the names of the tenants, though if letting room by room, this may be hard to get them to agree to. Appointing a "head tenant" who pays the bills and who can be trusted can work well, often in exchange for a lower rent.

55

Finally, in some house shares, including those for students, the tenants may live in the same accommodation as you, the owner of the property. In this situation, they are effectively lodgers and they will not have an assured shorthold tenancy. The status of the lodger in such an arrangement is sometimes described as that of an "excluded occupier" and the arrangement often referred to as an "excluded license". It is *excluded* because it is excluded from the protections that exist in a tenancy agreement and it is a *license,* because they have been given a license to live there for a period. But really, their rights are very limited indeed. If someone lives in your home as a lodger, the agreement they have will be informal and is not an assured shorthold tenancy. The deposit (if there is one) does not therefore need to be protected in a tenancy deposit scheme. In many lodger arrangements, a lot of bills may be included within the rent - such as council tax, water, electricity and gas bills as well as broadband, TV, phone and TV license. Make sure you are clear about what's included and what isn't. Lodger agreements are available online. Just do a quick search. You should follow the same steps to collect references as set out in Chapter 2.

Letting to Local Authorities, Housing Associations and Other Government Agencies

This might surprise some people but, yes, the local authorities, the housing associations and some other government agencies will pay you rent directly for your property. (We reckon that as much as around 2 per cent of all privately let residential property is let this way).

"Really?" I hear you ask. "Why and how do councils and housing associations do this?"

Well, to understand this, here's a short history lesson.

If you live in London and the South East you may have noticed we have a bit of a housing shortage. Sure, other areas have housing shortages in some shape or form too - but not as bad as that which exists in London and the so called "Home Counties".

The people who often find it hardest to get accommodation are those who tend to have the lowest incomes as well as those whose personal housing or other background is, well, "more colourful".

Now I could go on about the politics of this for a long time, but suffice to say, the responsibility for the fact that those who are poor and often have the greatest unmet housing needs must lie, in part, with the government - governments of both hues are guilty.

After the Second World War we had a really bad housing crisis, a lot of it caused by a certain Austrian with a moustache. Yet despite the fact that the UK government was hugely in debt to our pals across the pond, (and a lot worse off than we are today), we somehow still managed to build lot of new housing - a lot of it municipal or, as it came to be known, council housing.

And then along came Margaret Thatcher, a true blue "all British people should own their own homes advocate" to sell off a lot of the council stock at knock down prices. Her policies were followed by other Conservative governments and also Labour ones too, though Labour struggles to match the Conservatives for their ability to throw tax payers cash at first time buyers to the delight of their pals in the UK's biggest housebuilding firms.

And so, the deed has now been done - much of the council stock has been sold off and it cannot be reversed, resulting in a shortage of the sort of low cost social housing that folks on low incomes would once have lived in. (Note: "Social housing" somehow became the new politically correct word for council housing at some time in the 90s, probably around the time when housewives and, um, house husbands also became domestic engineers).

The problem of lack of housing in general, and affordable housing in particular, has been exacerbated by the big rises in the UK population in recent years (mainly as a result of migration but also due to increased life expectancy and divorce rates). And so we now have ever longer waiting lists for council housing. We have a full blown housing crisis in some parts of the UK - every bit as bad as it was post World War 2.

A few years ago the government sort of gave up on the idea of council (sorry, social) housing and said to people on the now massively long waiting list, that they would have to accept offers of accommodation in the private rented sector. And if they did not accept these, then it was tough but the local councils would not be under any further obligation to help them further.

So, there is it - and that's how the private rented sector often became the main option for those on low incomes whose choices in housing were fewest.

In order to afford to pay rents, people on low incomes or no incomes often have to look to the government to help them with the money for the rent and to have some semblance of what society deems to be a "normal life".

And so, people can apply for (and providing their circumstances do not preclude them), may be entitled to what is still generically known as "housing benefit".

As well as giving housing benefit to some people who then use it to pay rent to their landlord, there is another way that the government and other bodies get involved directly with some very vulnerable groups of people who are in really desperate need of housing.

The smart thing (from the landlords point of view) is that for these very desperate people, money to cover their rent can be paid *directly from the government* and other "blue chip" bodies such as housing associations - and it is guaranteed week after week, month after month for up to five years.

Yes, you read that correctly - they, the government and the housing associations will pay you, the landlord directly.

Now, you'll recall how I just mentioned that these days the local authorities could make offers of accommodation in the private rented sector to someone on the council waiting list and if that person turned down such reasonable offers repeatedly, the council could, as they put it, "discharge their duty to house that person" - effectively saying, "We can't help you, mate."

That is true, up to a point. They can do this.

However, there are some circumstances where the council simply has to step in and find emergency, temporary accommodation for certain people. A good example will be a mother with young children who have nowhere to live. Society has not got so harsh (yet) that it is comfortable with seeing mothers and young children sleeping on the street. (It's OK for young single men and women to sleep on the streets or try their luck at hostels but not kids, not yet!)

And so, there is an ever present need for temporary accommodation for such people (and some other very vulnerable groups too). The requirement for such urgently needed accommodation varies from council to council - and it's fair to say that the more urban and / or deprived the area is, the greater the need tends to be.

So this is what happens: Local authorities and housing associations run programmes where they offer to lease properties from private landlords for fairly long periods - ranging from 18 months to five years - which they use to house vulnerable people on a "temporary basis". Some other government agencies may also offer leases too - for example, the department that deals with asylum seekers has a similar scheme - but mostly it is councils and housing associations that do this.

Under these leases, your "tenant" will be the local authority or housing association who will then effectively sub-let your property to house the people who are in real need. In return for this, they will pay you a guaranteed rent for the duration of the lease.

How much you get in rent is linked to whatever the housing benefit rate is for that area and for the size of property, less a small amount as a management fee to cover them for minor repairs, (which they will generally attend to free of charge), and to cover their work to administer the scheme.

The amount of the rent you'll get is usually set at the outset of the lease for the entire duration of the lease, though in some cases, there may be inflation linked adjustments.

This sounds quite a compelling offer - and in many ways it is.

1. You get a guaranteed rent for a long period and it is paid by a local authority or housing association, which means there is zero risk of the rent not being paid.

2. As the rent is guaranteed, whether there is anyone in your property or not, you do not have to worry too much about periods when the property is empty (called "void periods" in landlords jargon).

3. There will be no letting and management fees to pay.

4. The local authority or housing association will often look after minor repairs as part of their contract with you. (Check the contract carefully because not all have such generous terms.)

5. You may not have to furnish the property as many local authorities and housing associations prefer the properties they lease to be unfurnished. This will save you money on buying and replacing furnishings, reduce the cost of any inventory checks you have to have done and cut insurance costs too.

It all sounds very good. However, there are some drawbacks to such schemes which mean they may not be to the liking of all landlords.

Firstly, as mentioned above, the rent level in these schemes will always be a little below "market rents". Come on! You are getting a guaranteed rent from a blue chip body - the government. What more do you want? Blood?

In some cases, the rents may well be considerably below what you could get if you found a tenant "in the open market" who was willing to rent it from you. Rates are always linked to the level of housing benefits.

These days, housing benefits are subjected to overall maximum caps (very relevant in London) and they can anyway be no more than the "thirtieth percentile of local reference rents". Therefore the amounts paid will be very much at the bottom end of local rent levels.

Second, and this is a biggie - you have no control over who the local authority or housing association puts in your property. None at all. Now this might not matter to you much, but it might matter a lot to the neighbours who live close to the property being leased in this way. The fact is that the people being housed under such schemes are homeless and in desperate need of a roof over their heads. Some will be deserving cases and will be as good as gold. Some stay for a long time. However, it has to be said that many people are in desperate circumstances partly because of bad choices of their own making.

For example, the nice Mum and kid, who the council have housed in your property may well get visited by the drunken, drug crazed man they were once living with (the Mum's past bad choice, possibly, discuss!) and who they are now seeking shelter from. And yes, he may cause some damage or some commotion. And yes, the Mum may be daft enough to let him back in. And yes, he might get drunk again and smash up your place and annoy the hell out of neighbours.

These kind of risks are sadly higher among people who are poor, vulnerable and especially those in urgent need of accommodation. The bad stuff that happens to them and to the places they live in may not be their fault, but the chances of the bad stuff happening are much higher than they are in the general population who get the 0810hrs fast train from Sidcup each morning to an office job in the City.

Third, some mortgage lenders don't allow these kinds of sublet, though for landlords that don't tell their lender, the chances of being found out may be pretty slim. (Of course, if you don't have a mortgage, this won't concern you). More relevant, possibly, is the insurance position. Some insurance companies may charge higher premiums where a property is sublet in this way, partly because they don't like properties to be empty and partly because they know that the risks of damages and claims are that much higher. And if the property is a flat, it's worth checking that such an arrangement, (where the underlying sub-tenants might come and go), is not in breach of the provisions in the lease (which often require a longer term tenancy).

Fourth, dealing with your local authority or housing association can be rather trying. Despite the nature of what they are trying to do - finding accommodation urgently for people in need, they can be remarkably bureaucratic, slow at making decisions and tardy at even coming to see if your property is suitable. OK, before folks at the housing associations write to me to complain, a lot of the reasons for the tardiness may be due to lack of resourcing following cuts to their budgets from central government.

Due to their public standing and fear of adverse publicity, many local authorities and housing associations insist on the very highest standards too. This is fair enough, but their requirements often go far above and beyond what you would have to do in any normal "market let". So you might have to spend money making modifications to your property which you would otherwise not need to do. As an example of this, on one lease scheme which I entered into, the housing association bizarrely insisted that we had to put in a brand new toilet seat, even though there was nothing wrong with the one that was there already. Weird!

Fifth, you still need to be "on their case" to check the quality of their property management, which can be mixed at best. Most will have some sort of "Care Scheme" whereby they or their nominated provider will carry out minor repairs free of charge. However, if the boiler breaks (and they deem you need a new one) or there is a leak in the roof, these types of major repairs and fixes will not usually be covered, so you'll have to pay for the fix anyway. So check the detail of the contract, OK?

The housing association lease scheme which let one of my properties back in 2001 had a cover scheme with a certain large utility company, who carried out minor fixes to boilers as part of their contract. One fine day, back in 2004, the housing association contacted me and said I'd need a new boiler at a cost of three thousand pounds. Instead, I got my own engineer out who did a fix for £60 - and twelve years later the same boiler is still going just fine. (Yes, I could write another book about these "service contracts" from the likes of the big utility companies, but that is another story).

In practice, the type of property that might suit these kinds of leases to local authorities and housing associations are the types of homes that are perhaps at the lower end of the market, for example on estates of a rougher hue or on more downmarket streets, where the landlord may struggle to achieve market level rents otherwise and where he will be happy with the rent level (and guarantee) offered by the local authority / housing association.

Also, given the enhanced risk of antisocial behaviour it is probably best if the neighbours are not the sensitive type who will complain if the ex-boyfriend and part time "Dad" of the single Mum's kids comes round drunk and makes a lot of noise. If they are of such a disposition, think hard whether it's a good idea that the neighbours have your phone number (and never give out a phone number that cannot be switched off at the weekend or at night).

The greatest demand for properties under these schemes are for one bed or two bed houses. That is because the greatest need for urgent accommodation tends to be from Mums with one or two kids. "Mums with Kids" represents the main group that the local authorities have to find accommodation for urgently.

So, how do you find out about such schemes?

Well, the first thing is the terminology. The lease schemes are often called "local authority or council private rented leasing schemes" or "housing association private rented leasing schemes". However, they may be called other names locally.

A good starting place to look is on the local authority website under the housing section. For the housing associations, we suggest you google "housing associations guaranteed rent" + "your area" or just "guaranteed rent + your area". (It is worth noting that many London boroughs are seeking accommodation under such schemes in far flung parts of the country, so even if you are in Wrexham, you might end up with a lease with a London council).

Not all housing association and local government websites are kept updated regularly though and you might do well to call them and try to make sure you are speaking to the right

65

department - which will usually be something to do with "private housing".

Then make sure you check the terms and conditions of the lease scheme very carefully. And do read all the small print, yes, all of it! Find out how fast the operator of the scheme can come to see your property, which they will always need to do, before they can take it onto the scheme. Despite the urgent need, you'd be surprised that it can take weeks for them to fix an appointment - a sad reflection of their lack of manpower or maybe their inefficiency. Discuss!

If they insist on a whole lot of modifications to your property to meet their standards, you could be facing quite a long void period whilst you get the work done. So that is why we say you should have a clear understanding of what they might need done to meet their requirements. Maybe they insist just on new toilet seats or maybe the standards will be more demanding. So find out first - to save your time and theirs.

Finally a word of warning. There are many private companies around who may contact you and claim to be "working for the council" or even "working with them as contractors" to "find accommodation for tenants and then paying guaranteed rent to you". Some will even use the council's own logos on their websites.

Be warned, these are mostly scam companies operating what is really known in the trade as "rent to rent" operations. They will rent your place from you and then fill up with tenants who "come from the council" only in the sense that they are usually on housing benefit.

Get into bed with one of these operators, and your rent is only guaranteed as long the company who runs the scheme does not go bust. Many of these companies are scams in the first place and you'll get no rent at all, ever. Many others have operated schemes for a while and then gone bust, leaving you with tenants in your property, whose names you do not even know and who don't even know of your existence. Naturally, they are all on benefits but paying you no rent. Mmm, not a nice situation - and don't expect the council to help you out or to start paying you direct, even if they once were making payments to the now bust company that set up the scheme! They won't talk to you and will cite the Data Protection Act as the reason for not wanting to get involved!

So, for goodness sake do not enter into such arrangements with these scam private companies. Stick to dealing only with local authorities and the housing associations, whose rent payments to you are *really* guaranteed.

Letting Directly to Tenants on Housing Benefit / Local Housing Allowance / Universal Credit

The other way that you can get involved in letting to people on housing benefits, is by letting to them directly.

Yes, you'll have gathered from the previous section that it's my opinion that tenants whose housing options are fewest, including those on low incomes and benefits have had a pretty bad time as a result of recent government policies.

As well as the changes I described there, the government has also stopped paying landlords direct and many private landlords did not like it, because back in the old days, the tenants could elect for the housing benefit to be paid directly to you. Indeed, many tenants preferred the money going straight to their landlord, because it meant the money was effectively "ring fenced" to some extent - removing the natural temptation for the tenant to spend it on something else. And, naturally, many landlords liked it that way too - as they were more certain of receiving the money.

The change to set the amount of housing benefit that could be claimed to a level equal to the 30th percentile of local rents (previously it was at the 50th percentile or median) and to set a maximum cap on the amount of housing benefit that any family could claim had some merits and change was probably needed but, once again, it also served to make this end of the market even less attractive for landlords.

Another factor that has always worried landlords is that dealing with the benefit end of the market can be time consuming in terms of administration. Landlords rightly worry that there is lots of paperwork - and that the payment system can often mess things up and they will not receive rent as a consequence, or if they do receive it, it comes in late. The sad thing about this is that it is, of course, the tenants who are caught in the middle.

The very latest government initiative was to bring in the Universal Credit system. This new system, the brainchild of Ian Duncan Smith MP, is a system of a single payment for all benefit entitlements, which includes within it, the housing benefit element. This is being rolled out across the UK in 2015 and 2016. Another change, another chance for things to get messed up - well, that is how many landlords see this new initiative.

The Chief Executive of one of the largest online letting agents tells me that around 95 per cent of the landlords who place adverts on his site, now specify "No Housing Benefit / No Universal Credit".

So, given all these worries, should landlords still consider letting to people on housing benefit?

Well, the answer is still Yes. And the marketing approach can follow the same routes as explained in Chapter 2 - either using an online letting agent or a high street letting agent (providing the high street agent accepts such lets).

Of course, the applicants will have a low income or may not be employed at all - so there may be no need to seek employment references. Instead, you might want to consider requesting a guarantor instead - and then do the reference checks on them, just as you would for any tenant applicant.

Here are our tips for making lettings to people on housing benefit work well.

First, applicants should apply for housing benefit as soon as they are eligible - and also, within their application, they should give the "OK" to the housing benefit officer to discuss their application with you, at application stage and ongoing. This will ensure that you are not "out of the loop" and that you have the necessary information on how things are progressing. This will be of significant assurance because if rent payments stop, because the housing benefit has been stopped or reduced or delayed, at least you'll be able to verify why this has happened and find out when payments will be re-started by speaking directly to the housing benefit officer.

Second, remember the amount of housing benefit depends on the area the home is in and also the tenants' needs. So, a single mum or couple with a child, will not get enough benefit for a three bed flat. And if the applicant is under 35, they will only get enough for a room in a shared house.

Third, some local authority's housing benefit departments can be very slow at processing claims. So if payment is delayed ask the paying authorities for an interim payment, which they must make within 14 days of having the necessary information they need from you.

Fourth, if the local authority deems the applicant "vulnerable" or if they are getting assistance from the local authority, (perhaps they have assisted the case by issuing a bond to a landlord in lieu of the fact that the applicant doesn't have enough cash for a deposit), you may still be able to get payments of rent made directly to you, as part of a system that's usually known as "safeguarding". Payments can also be made directly to the landlord if the tenant is two months' in arrears of rent, though naturally, you don't want to ever be in this position.

Fifth, the fact is that, on average, people who are benefit dependent stay longer than other types of tenant. And that is what most sensible landlords want, as changeovers of tenants cost money. The problems with housing benefit, where they do occur, often arise in the set up stage, but once they are set up, they tend to work OK.

Other help may be available from the council too. So find out what's out there. Examples include:

1. "Fast tracking" of payment of housing benefit. The schemes can work closely with the housing benefit people to make sure the paperwork is right first time and prioritise payments - often making payments direct to you too.

2. Making a named contact available locally to talk to both you and the tenant to resolve any issues.

3. Giving help to the tenant in term of training on matters such as how to look after a property properly, sort out minor issues and help with budgeting. Also, ongoing support once the tenancy has started to make sure it is sustained.

4. Making deposits, deposit guarantees (bonds) and rent in advance and other incentives available to you. This is particularly important for landlords as many tenants at this end of the market will not have enough money to pay a four or six week deposit, unless they happen to know a willing home-owning guarantor. Also, tenants at this end of the market probably will not be able to pay the first months' rent in advance because the benefits system may not have made the first payment in time for the tenancy start date. So, for this reason, deposits, bonds, rent in advance payments and incentive payments to landlords (which can be as much as three months' rent in London) can all be appealing and reduce the risk and cash flow problems.

Many of these "access schemes" are only available for certain groups - for example, people who are on the council (social) housing waiting list, families with young children or perhaps people who have suffered from drug and alcohol problems, people coming out of prison or other vulnerable groups.

The schemes vary greatly across different boroughs and are subject to change over time as a result of changes in central and town hall politics and funding.

Some schemes are run by local councils or by trusts set up by councils, whilst others are managed by charities. It is up to you to find out what is available in your area. Start your search online, including at the local authority's website. But also make phone enquiries too as not all councils are good at keeping their websites up-to-date.

At my consultancy, I have helped many councils design private rented sector access schemes that work effectively. It is a shame that too many schemes we have seen, despite high hopes for them, don't work as well as they should - and many are pretty abject and have been abandoned altogether. The main weakness is that the originators do not understand how to market effectively to private landlords to get them interested in signing up. This is a shame because many of the schemes have great incentives for landlords and tenants. But unless landlords can be made aware of them, they are bound to fail.

The landlords most likely to consider joining a private rented access scheme and /or letting to people on benefits tend to be more experienced and often they have more than one property and have been letting for a while. The more "accidental landlord" who is letting their former home, tends to find dealing with the housing benefit system too challenging, cumbersome and difficult, so they tend to leave well alone, (like the 95% of landlords who use the online letting agency I mentioned).

Whether you decide to let to benefit-dependent tenants will depend very much on where the property is and what kind of property it is too. Also, whether you are "up" for what might be a more challenging let, at least at the outset.

The fact is, if you get the right sort of tenant, it is often a good thing. The fact is there are good tenants who depend entirely on benefits and there are rubbish ones. Equally, there are good tenants who are on high incomes and there are tenants on high incomes whom you would not wish on your worst enemy.

The key point is, whoever the tenant is, you still have to do thorough reference checks - and if they cannot afford it on their own, you will have to see if they can provide a suitably checked and referenced guarantor, or maybe get help with their deposit from a private rented sector access scheme, or both.

If you are still not convinced of their ability to pay or to be good tenants, my advice is to not let to them. Don't take the risk. End of story.

The reality of the situation with benefit tenants is that there are some areas of the country, some estates where you will be waiting a long, long time to get a tenant who isn't dependent on housing benefits. These are the unemployment blackspots, the poor estates.

If you have a property in such a neighbourhood it is unlikely to appeal to a non-housing benefit dependent tenant, and you don't have much choice in the matter. Your options will either to be to let direct to tenants who are dependent on housing benefit or to a housing association or council under a lease scheme (if they run any locally). But the reality is that on the rougher estates, the probability of having a bad tenant will be that much higher.

Outside of bad neighbourhoods and rough estates, the risk of a housing benefit dependent tenant turning out to be bad is probably no higher than a tenant who is not dependent on benefits turning out to be bad. I have seen no clear statistical evidence that they are better or worse. All you can do is carry out the appropriate reference checks to weed out the potential bad tenants and avoid them.

The only thing that is a sure thing is the additional bureaucracy and potential delay in rental payments being made. There is not much you can do about this, except to keep an open dialogue with the tenant and the paying authority and if there are delays, take matters up with whoever administers the payments.

Appendix - "About the Property and the Contract"

This is the document that is referred to in the text in Chapter 2 called "About the Property and the Contract". It is the attachment document that goes with the email that we send to people once we have provisionally booked for them to come to a viewing of our property. More information about this document is in Chapter 2.

Dear Mrs, XXXXXX,

Thanks for your enquiry about our property at 1 Abbott View, Corbyn Road, Islington N1 0XX.

The property is in a quiet road in an up and coming area, near lots of shops, restaurants and the station.

Links to the property entry at Rightmove are here: XXXXXXXX

Various links to some information on the area can be found here: XXXXXXX

We'd like to have you as our tenant but first we think it is useful if you can read some more info about the property.

So we've included here all the info you need, including the references we require from you, should you wish to rent the property.

The types of references we need are pretty standard across all letting businesses. In the notes below, we explain why we need them, when we need them and what the steps are leading up to moving in.

It is quite a bit to read but we hope by explaining it all clearly here, you know what to do right from the start.

However, if you have a question, please contact me *during normal business hours.* I can be contacted on this number - Tel: 07XXX XXXX Email: XXXXXXXXXXX

Who am I? I am Jo Bloggs, I together with Mrs. Daphne Bloggs are the owners and landlords of the property. I deal with all matters connected with letting the property and all management of the property, 1 Abbott View, Corbyn Road, Islington, London N20 0XX.

What is (Insert name of Online Letting Agent) Acme Online Letting Agent is an online letting agent who I use to get our properties onto Rightmove, Zoopla and the other big property portals. Acme have sent us your details by email. I progress all matters from receipt of your enquiry onwards.

Kind regards

David Lawrenson

QUALIFYING CRITERIA

- We are sorry but this property is NOT available to Housing Benefit (Local Housing Allowance) dependent tenants.

The property would ideally suit 1 or 2 couples or a couple and up to 2 children, or three sharers under a single assured shorthold tenancy agreement (in which individuals have joint and several liability *for the whole rent).*

- You must be in employment and either rented before recently OR owned a property in the UK.

- You must show us that you have regular employment related gross income of at least 2.25 times the amount of the rent. Sight of your last 3 months' bank statements (or 6 months for self-employed applicants) will be required to verify this.

- If you are an applicant from a non-European Union or non-EEA state you must show a valid work permit to work in the United Kingdom and this must be valid for a further 2 years, or be extendable for at least this period of time.

- References from all applicants will be required.

- Deposit amount required (as detailed in our advert)

- We do not accept pets.

Please note, if you do not meet these criteria, we will not be able to let this property to you.

For more information on what documents and references we need, please read the sections below.

Please note this property is UNFURNISHED except for the following moveable main furnishing items only:

[LIST ITEMS IN THE PROPERTY]

Council TAX BAND is X and we understand the Council tax for this property is £X per annum.

For full details and pictures, see the adverts on Rightmove or Zoopla. Please note, we may occasionally use historic pictures that do not reflect the current state and condition of the property nor the furnishings that will be in the property on move in date.

Properties will be cleaned before your move in. Please note we will let the property in the state and condition that it was in when you viewed it and after being suitably cleaned. However, unless agreed with you in writing beforehand or in our marketing, the property will NOT be newly decorated.

We normally have no restrictions about tenants re-decorating - it is your home! However, you will need our sign off first

About the Rent and References Required

Note: Unlike most letting agents and some private landlords, we don't think you should have to pay excessive charges to take on a tenancy. Many letting agents charge up to £500 for reference checks, compiling tenancy agreements and other "entry costs" as well as tenancy renewal fees every 6 months. Some even require you to pay monthly "admin" fees too. We think this is unfair and excessive.

So the only charges we make are the following:

- *References - £50 for the first person and £35 for each other adult. (see later) This fee is payable by bank transfer to us before the referencing checks can start. We will only ask for this fee once you have sent us the documents that we need. Please note this fee is not refundable even if the credit report and reference checks mean we are unable to make you an offer of a tenancy. If we allow guarantors, they will have to pay £50 for the same, this is in addition to the charge for the tenants. The guarantor will be subjected to same checks as tenant applicants. Guarantors must be UK homeowners.*

- *Inventory - £100. This is only paid after references have been checked and a holding Reservation Fee has* been requested. It is paid at the same time as the Reservation fee is requested.

- *Reservation Fee equal to 3 weeks' rent. <u>You don't have to pay this now.</u> Only once references are checked and an offer to let made by us and accepted by you, will you be asked to pay a Reservation Fee as proof of your commitment to proceed. <u>This is returned in full to you when you have moved in and at the same time as you pay the deposit and first month's rent.</u>*

- *The deposit is as detailed in our advert. Your deposit which will be protected in the tenancy deposit scheme managed by Mydeposits. For more info see: **www.mydeposits.co.uk**.In some cases, a higher deposit amount may be required.*

Rent. This is £XXXXX per calendar month

- <u>*We do NOT charge annual renewal fees or monthly tenancy fees.*</u>*Once the tenancy is set up we only charge you the rent, that's it. However, if at any time there is a proposed change of tenant on the agreement, referencing charges of £50 will apply per new tenant, and in addition, if that applicant is successful, a new tenancy and a check out / check in inventory will need to be issued - the cost of this is an additional £220. Change of tenant will need to be agreed by us first and any new tenant must pass our referencing checks.*

Of course, in addition to the rent you will have to pay for council tax, electricity and gas, water, TV licence and you are liable to pay <u>all charges</u> in respect of the installation, setting up of and the connection of any phone, TV or broadband line. It is strongly recommended that you also take out your own contents insurance, including Accidental Damage Cover.

Property Available from Date is: DD / MM / YY, though the date may vary by a few days. We will accept start dates up to no later than DD/MM/YY.

The Tenancy Agreement contract between us will be a single assured shorthold tenancy. Minimum: 6 month term.

Rent adjustment will occur every 12 months.

If the tenancy has gone well, we will nearly **always** offer to extend it. Indeed, many of our tenants have been with us for years - and you are welcome to ask them about what we are like as landlords.

When the contract is extended beyond the initial 6 months, the notice period you will be required to give when you wish to leave will be a minimum of one calendar month.

Where there is to be more than one tenant, all tenants are jointly, severally and individually liable for the whole rent under a single contract.

Check the draft Tenancy Agreement for detailed terms of the tenancy (which we can send you on request if you are interested in going ahead to the reference stage).

Here is the link to the government produced "How to Rent" guide which you might find useful:
https://www.gov.uk/government/publications/how-to-rent

Why We Need to Seek References and Check Documents

In the same way as when you apply for a loan, when you apply to become a tenant you will find that all professional landlords and letting agents in the UK will check to see that you can afford to comfortably pay the rent.

We would normally expect gross combined tenants' employment income to be at least 2.25 times the rental income for the property and for you to be in a solvent position.

To help evaluate this and other facts about you, it is normal to ask you to supply certain simple references and documents to us. And in addition to these we also ask for proof of identity - which is why we ask to see your passport.

In the notes below I explain more fully what references and documents we need to see - plus the next steps leading to the granting of a tenancy.

We know our properties are competitively priced, so there is a lot of demand for them. Therefore, once you have seen the property and if you are interested in going ahead we ask **you** to produce the references we require as quickly as possible - preferably before the end of the next working day, to avoid disappointment.

We ask you to get the references and documents because we find it much easier and faster to ask you to obtain the references rather than us having to chase for them.

Please note that until ALL satisfactory references and documents are received and checked by us, **we cannot under any circumstances "hold" the property for you and the property will continue to be marketed to other tenants.** So, please move quickly to avoid disappointment.

If you are unable to supply one of the references, an alternative might be acceptable - so, if you have a problem, let us know.

References and Documents Required from You

The information, documents and references, which should be bought, emailed or sent to us at our offices, at XXXXXXXX [insert address] are as follows:

For the application to start, we need:

- your full name(s) (including any middle names)
- Date of birth and addresses (including full postcodes) for the last three years.
- **We also need the following:**

1. Sight of each page of your last 3 months original bank statements (or 6 months if you are self- employed) showing your address and incoming salary or other receipts (and your rent or mortgage payments going out). If your bank statement does not contain your current address, we will also need to see the last three months of an original billing statement which does - electricity OR gas OR phone bill in your name is an acceptable alternative. Bank statements must show the whole of each months' transactions. If you bank or pay utilities on line and do not have paper copies of statements you are welcome to bring your PC and bring up your bank statements on line at our offices.

2. **EITHER...** (If you are not self-employed): A Letter from a senior manager or HR officer at your employer. (Personnel departments are familiar with these requests and should be able to produce an appropriate letter immediately on request.)

The letter must state: a) How long you have been an employee b) the nature of your employment contract - e.g. permanent / temporary etc. c) your salary d) that you are not under notice of redundancy. They may address this letter "To Whom It May Concern" and give it to you for passing to us.

A recent contract of employment dated in the last month may be an acceptable alternative, at our discretion.

OR .... (If you are self-employed), we will need to see your last 6 months recent bank statements.

3. A Letter from your current or a recent landlord or letting agent. Ideally, this should include the one before your current landlord. This must state: a) start and end dates of tenancy and rent amount expressed in amount per month b) whether this rent was always paid on time c) whether there were any arrears in rent or complaints regarding antisocial behaviour d) whether they would recommend you as being a reliable, honest and trustworthy tenant. e) whether they would let to you again. If you are unable to obtain such letter, please advise me. An alternative may be acceptable.

4. A recent clear photograph of yourself (not a copy).

5. Sight of your passport as proof of your ID

AND if these documents are all OK, we will then need your authority to allow me to undertake a credit reference check and for checking the references.

The cost of referencing checking is £50 for the first adult. The second and subsequent adults will pay £35 each. This fee is payable by bank transfer or cash to us before the referencing can start**.** Please note this fee is <u>not refundable</u> even if the credit report and reference checks mean we are unable to make you an offer of a tenancy.

Depending on your circumstances we may also require the following:

1. If your employer does not pay your salary straight into your bank, we will need to additionally see your last 6 months original pay slips.

2. If you are not a citizen of an EEA country, (the European Union states plus the states of Switzerland, Lichtenstein, Norway and Iceland) we will need to have sight of your permit or visa entitling you to work in the United Kingdom for at least the next two years.

Note on References

The references and documentation listed above is required in respect of **each** tenant (if there are to be more than one tenant).

If you currently own your own home and are currently living there or have lived there up to the last 3 months, we may not need a landlord reference.

IMPORTANT: If you do not provide all the information we need we will not be able to process your application. If more than one applicant, all applicants will need to attend a meeting so we can check ID, which will be held in normal business hours between 9 and 5pm Monday to Friday.

Next Steps after References Have Been Checked

If all the documentation and references are satisfactory and fully validated along with ID validation, we will send you by email, a draft copy of the tenancy agreement for you to check, though we can send this earlier on request. You should check the agreement carefully and let us know if there are any terms you do not understand.

It is expected that you will have read the draft tenancy agreement BEFORE MOVE IN DAY (as there will NOT be sufficient time to read it in detail on move in day.)

If you wish to go ahead, we will agree a planned move in date and to ensure your commitment and you will be asked to pay a holding Reservation Fee equivalent to 3 weeks rent as proof of your commitment to proceed plus the cost of the detailed inventory for the property, which is £100.

This can be paid in cash or, if you prefer, it can be paid by immediate bank transfer - however, we **must** be in receipt of cleared funds. (The holding reservation fee will be deducted from the first month rent which is paid on the day you move in.)

Once we have the Reservation Fee the property will be taken off the market.

IMPORTANT: If you are unable to pay the Reservation Fee within 24 hours of us making an offer of a tenancy, we will commence re-marketing the property and you risk losing the property to someone else.

Please note that if you change your mind prior to move in day for any reason whatsoever or, if on move in date, you are unable to pay 1) The balance of the first months' rent (defined as the first months' rent less holding reservation fee) AND 2) The full amount of the deposit, then you will lose the holding reservation fee.

Steps before Move-in Date

You must make the following preparations:

- Contact electricity, water, gas and phone and broadband providers to set up your account and to ensure that the service is switched on when you move in. You are responsible for all connection service costs that may be applied by the telephone / broadband provider.

- Also, contact Council Tax Tel 00000000 and website **www.XXXXXXX.gov.uk**.

- Make arrangements to set up your own contents insurance. This should include accidental damage cover.

On Move-in day - Meet at the Property

On or before move in day, you will need to have paid the whole of the first months' rent (less the Reservation Fee) plus the deposit.

The total sum required must be paid in cash or we must be in receipt of cleared funds via inter-bank Chaps transfer before the move in day.

Your deposit will be protected in the tenancy deposit scheme operated by Mydeposits.co.uk - and you will sent confirmation of this and an explanation of the scheme. As part of the scheme's requirements, we will need an alternative postal address for you.

On move in day, we will meet at the property at an agreed time - which must be between 9am and 4pm Mon to Friday. **We do not work on Saturdays or on Sundays.**

You must allow at least one 1 hour to complete formalities at the property. You will be shown how the facilities at the property work and given time to make any additional notes and observations on the inventory (the list and state & condition of furnishings), record meter readings and be given all the information you need to enjoy the house.

You will not be able to move in any belongings or receive the house keys until these formalities have been completed.

A video and photos may be taken to back up the inventory, which will be carried out by an **inventory clerk appointed by us.** You will be given a copy of the inventory report within 2 weeks of move in date.

We will sign the Tenancy agreement contract including the inventory (if a printed version is available already) and you will sign for the keys. (Any amendments to the inventory or comments that you, as the tenant make can be added later.)

Please note if there is to be more than one tenant on the contract **ALL tenants must attend on move in date to sign the contract.**

Arranging for Payments after Move-in Date - Payments for Ongoing Rent

You must set up your standing order in good time.

The payment for the rent for the next month after the start date of the agreement must be in my account as cleared funds by the "month anniversary" of the date you moved in. So, for example, suppose you moved in on 8th of September, the next rent payment would be due in my account by 8th October. To ensure that this happens you should instruct your bank to make sure

87

that the first standing order payment leaves your account on the 3rd October and then each 3rd of each month. This 5 day period will allow sufficient time for funds to be cleared (including an allowance for the delaying effect of weekends and other bank holidays.)

If there is more than one tenant the rent payments **must be made by a single standing order** for the full amount each month.

Settling In

On or before the day you move in, we will show you that the smoke and carbon monoxide alarms work and we will show you where the gas and electric safety certificates are. We will give you a copy of the energy performance report too, together with a copy of the document produced by the government called, "How to Rent."

We will also give you all necessary proscribed information about the tenancy deposit scheme along with a signed certificate for the deposit, which we request you sign and return to us.

(These are legal requirements that we must comply with for Assured Shorthold Tenancy types of agreement).

For maintenance, we have a team of people you can call. We are not plumbers nor are we electricians nor heating engineers. But we have people who are, who work for us. You will be given their contact details, which are included at the end of the tenancy agreement.

In the event of a breakdown, fault or service requirement, please call them as appropriate. Only call us to let us know if a tradesman fails to respond or attend an appointment. We will then take over and deal with the matter for you.

Please do call us if you don't understand anything here. We look forward to meeting you.

Kind Regards

END OF DOCUMENT

Printed in Great Britain
by Amazon